A LAWYER'S CASE
FOR THE
RESURRECTION

AUTHOR OF
A Lawyer's Case for God & A Lawyer's Case for His Faith

JIM JACOB, ESQ.

To read this booklet online for free or to purchase it, please visit JimJacobBooks.com. It is also available on Amazon.

For bulk pricing of quantities of 20 or more, please email Info@JimJacobBooks.com.

ISBN: 978-1-940164-40-3

Printed in the United States of America

A LAWYER'S CASE
FOR THE
RESURRECTION

A LAWYER'S CASE FOR THE RESURRECTION

INTRODUCTION

Is God just a figment of our imagination? Do only the most uneducated and naïve among us believe in God? Are Abraham, Isaac, Jacob, and Moses nothing more than fictional characters? Is the story of the resurrection of Yeshua (Jesus' Hebrew name) the greatest hoax of all time? For the first 39 years of my life when I was a Jewish atheist, I would have answered a resounding "Yes" to all of these questions.

I vowed that one day I would read the Bible to see what all the hoopla was about, but never did for many years. A few people shared with me the importance of following Yeshua, but it all sounded like irrational fanaticism. I vividly recall a Jewish classmate of mine in high school becoming a "Jesus freak" and wanting to show me the amazing things he had discovered in the Bible. I admired his passion, but was not the least bit interested in his offer.

As I began my legal career in 1978, I met more and more followers of Yeshua. I was genuinely shocked to learn that many highly skilled and analytical attorneys believed this "religious" stuff. I had always assumed that anyone with a faith in Yeshua was quite gullible. I have since learned that many renowned historians, scholars, and rabbis wholeheartedly embrace what I had previously considered preposterous. I had rejected belief in Yeshua without ever even learning what I was rejecting. One night, 23 years ago, I was asked if I would like to know Yeshua. I decided that I did want to know Him—*if* He was real. Since that night, I have learned that He is very real, and my life has never been the same.

For many years after I became a follower of Yeshua, I assumed that it was a matter of faith to believe that He was the Son of God who performed miracles and was resurrected from the dead. I have since learned that there is a significant amount of historically compelling evidence for the life, sacrificial death, and resurrection of Yeshua. I will share some of this evidence in the following pages.

Most of you probably picked up this booklet because you are interested in discovering (or perhaps refuting) whether there is valid historical evidence to prove the resurrection of Yeshua. However, before we can discuss the resurrection, we will need to develop a bit of a foundation.

First, we will review what followers of Yeshua believe. Then we will explore how historians prove history. Next we will determine whether the gospel writings (the first four books of the Bible's New Covenant which offer accounts of Yeshua's life, death, and resurrection) can be used as historical evidence. Then we will examine the evidence from ancient witnesses for His life and crucifixion. Lastly, we will analyze the historical evidence for the resurrection. Each section builds on one another, so I encourage you to read them in order. You may disagree with the persuasiveness of one piece of evidence; however, when viewing the evidence in its entirety, I believe the historical validity for the life, crucifixion, and resurrection of Yeshua is extremely compelling.

Ultimately, you are the judge and jury. At the conclusion of a trial, a jury reviews *all* of the evidence presented and renders a verdict. I ask you to do the same with the evidence presented for the life, death, and resurrection of Yeshua, the Jewish Messiah.

WHAT DO FOLLOWERS OF YESHUA BELIEVE?

Followers of Yeshua believe that He was a Jewish man who was born and lived in Israel approximately 2,000 years ago. His Hebrew name was Yeshua, which means "salvation." Yeshua preached in synagogues and performed miraculous healings in the presence of many witnesses. He claimed to be the Son of God, which the Jewish leaders considered blasphemous. When Yeshua was in His early 30s, the Romans, at the insistence of the Jewish leaders, had Him publicly crucified.

Prior to His death, Yeshua was flogged repeatedly with a whip containing metal and broken glass. Nails were then driven into His hands and feet, and He was crucified by being hung on an execution stake in the shape of a cross. After being pronounced dead, Yeshua was placed in a grave secured by a large stone and guarded by Roman soldiers. Despite this security, eyewitnesses found the tomb empty three days later! It is recorded that after His death Yeshua appeared to many people, including over 500 people at one time. Some of these witnesses are listed in the Bible and can be found in the gospels, the Book of Acts, and other books in the New Covenant (New Testament/Messianic Scriptures/Brit Chadasha).

The followers of Yeshua believe that He was God in the flesh, and the long awaited Messiah of Israel whose life, death, and resurrection had been foretold in many passages by Jewish Prophets in the Old Covenant (Old Testament/Hebrew Scriptures/Tanakh). As will be discussed, virtually all respected historians acknowledge the life, crucifixion, death, and burial of Yeshua.

DETERMINING HISTORICAL AUTHENTICITY

Before we can look at the historical evidence for the life of Yeshua, we need to understand how history is discovered. To help illuminate the process of historical authentication, let's first discuss how historians would prove the specific actions by a pilot at the Normandy Invasion during WWII. To begin, historians would probably go right to the source and interview available commanders, pilots, and other witnesses who interacted with the pilot. They would determine the authenticity of each narrative offered by comparing the stories to see whether they were significantly contradictory. These historians would attempt to gather any physical evidence that may refer to this pilot (e.g., letters and artifacts, as well as Air Force records). They would also search for any video footage or photographs that may validate the accounts told by the individuals.

If the pilot's actions were particularly heroic, there may be ample historical evidence available. Even if there were seemingly conclusive evidence proving what the pilot did during the Normandy Invasion, historians would be unable to verify what happened with absolute certainty. Despite the imagination of sci-fi writers, we cannot go back in time. Although evidence such as photographs, videos, and audio recordings may cause historians to assign extremely high probability to a historical event, nothing in history can be proved with 100% certainty. Historian Dr. Michael Licona describes the process of discovering both biblical and non-biblical history:

> When historians say "x occurred" in the past, they are actually claiming the following: *given the available data, the best explanation indicates that we are warranted*

in having a reasonable degree of certainty that x occurred and that it appears more certain at the moment than competing hypotheses. Accordingly we have a rational basis for believing it. However, our conclusion is subject to revision or abandonment, since new data may surface in the future showing things happened differently than presently proposed, (emphasis added).[1]

Obviously, historians cannot recreate history in a laboratory; instead, they scrutinize the available evidence to determine what occurred. This process becomes even more complex as they attempt to determine the validity of events from centuries ago.

How would historians validate the life and explorations of Christopher Columbus? Clearly, they would not be able to authenticate Columbus' journeys from Spain to the New World using video footage, audio recordings, or photographs. They would likewise be unable to interview Columbus, or any members of his crew. They would have to use the evidence available (most likely letters, other writings, and artifacts), and draw the conclusions most supported by the evidence.

There is rarely a single piece of evidence that conclusively corroborates a specific event or individual in ancient history. Rather, history is assembled in pieces, like a giant jigsaw puzzle, by using archeological discoveries, writings, and logic. As in a court of law, any theory is analyzed based on its consistency with the available evidence. Any purported statement by a witness is scrutinized with respect to their motive to lie, as well as the inconsistency of their testimony with the other available statements and evidence.

With historical events and individuals who lived thousands of years ago, we simply will not have the type of evidence that we have grown accustomed to in the 21st century. We cannot present conclusive evidence such as photographs, fingerprint analysis, or video footage to prove the historical authenticity of individuals who lived centuries ago. However, this lack of evidence does not mean that historians cannot establish events of the past to have high historical certainty.

Perhaps you feel like this has all been obvious information. You may reason, "Of course I understand that ancient history is discovered differently." But, we need to understand this means that the resurrection may have evidence some do not deem to be convincing enough. If you are reading this expecting to find 2,000-year-old scientific evidence (e.g., the discovery of the body of Yeshua), or one piece of evidence proving the resurrection of Yeshua occurred with 100% certainty, you will be disappointed because this is not the way that ancient history is determined. Understand though, if you are using this standard to measure the historical authentication of the life of Yeshua, you must be consistent and use this same standard for *all* of history, including the validation of historical figures such as Alexander the Great, Columbus, and Socrates.[2]

Ultimately, expecting to find evidence with 100% historical certainty will leave you unable to prove anything in history, as there is no such thing as historical *absolute* certainty. Although history cannot be proved with absolute certainty, historians are able to establish "historical facts," or events and evidence that have been deemed by the majority of scholars to have a very high degree of certainty. The evidence presented in the following pages validating the resurrection of Yeshua will be based on some of these historical facts and will be referred to as "Exhibits."

When establishing a historical fact, experts commonly use a method called "inference to the best explanation."[3] This process examines all available evidence and then uses this evidence to deduce the most likely explanation of what occurred in a given historical event. When using this process, historians look at the quantity, quality, and plausibility of the evidence, as well as the bias of the individual who is presenting the evidence. Ultimately, logic is applied to the available evidence to draw the conclusion of what most likely occurred in the past. I invite you to utilize this method of drawing the most reasonable conclusion based upon the available evidence for the life, death, and resurrection of Yeshua.

THE GOSPELS ARE HISTORICALLY CREDIBLE

The four historical accounts of the life of Yeshua in the Bible are some of the most useful pieces of evidence in determining His historicity. These four accounts—Matthew, Mark, Luke, and John—are known as the "gospels" and are the first four books of the New Covenant.[4] There is often debate as to whether the gospels can be utilized as a historical source. Some argue that because the gospels are in the Bible, they have no historical value. However, as will be shown, to demand only extra-biblical evidence to prove the historical validity of the resurrection of Yeshua is to demand historians to ignore some of the best available evidence.

To some, the question remains as to whether these texts can be relied upon as historical evidence. In the following section, we will review some of the more common objections against the historical validity of the New Covenant.

Claim 1: We Do Not Know What Was Originally Written
Claim 2: There are too Many Contradictions
Claim 3: There is No Non-Biblical Historical Evidence

In the following sections, we will then examine the evidence for the historical validity of the life, death, and resurrection of Yeshua.

Claim 1: We Do Not Know What Was Originally Written

Some presume the gospels are invalid because they were not written during the life of Yeshua. The majority of historians agree that the gospels were written 35-70 years following the death of Yeshua (which occurred in approximately 32 CE).[5] New Covenant scholar F.F. Bruce dates the writing of Mark to be shortly after 60 CE (approximately 28 years after the death of Yeshua), Luke between 60-70 CE[6], Matthew around 70 CE, and John between 90-100 CE.[7] The gospels were written in a time when hundreds of witnesses to Yeshua's ministry, life, death, and resurrection were still alive to refute or attest to the accuracy of the narratives.[8]

If all ancient historical facts required contemporaneous recordings (the recording of an event near to the time when it occurred), then we would not be able to prove much of *anything* about ancient history. For instance, we would be unable to prove the life of Alexander the Great if we held him to the same standard many hold for the life of Yeshua. The life of Alexander the Great is primarily proved using five sources. The *earliest* written evidence about his life was written around 40 CE, which is *363 years* following Alexander the Great's death.[9] It is found in a work by Quintus Curtius Rufus entitled *The History of Alexander*. That gap from the event to the recording of the event is over 300 years longer than the gospel writings about the life of Yeshua! Yet, few doubt that Alexander the Great lived and was one of the most brilliant military conquerors the world has ever seen. The expansive time span of the documentation of Alexander the Great's life does not invalidate the historical certainty that Alexander the Great truly lived. This is simply another example of how history is discovered. Despite one's theological beliefs, one must admit the life of Yeshua has far better *contemporaneous* historically documented written evidence than Alexander the Great.

Also, understanding the time in which the gospels were written enhances their credibility. Obviously, there was no printing press, so mass publication was impossible. Every copy was painstakingly written by hand, making writing extremely time consuming, expensive, and rather uncommon. The early followers of Yeshua were Jewish, and the gospels and New Covenant were all written by Jewish people (with the possible exception of the Gospel of Luke and the Book of Acts). As with the copying of the Old Covenant, the ancient Jewish scribes took immense care to ensure every letter, word, and line of the gospels and rest of the New Covenant were copied correctly.

This meticulous ancient Jewish practice has been verified through the discovery of the Dead Sea Scrolls in 1947. Before the discovery of these scrolls, the earliest manuscripts of the Old Covenant dated to around 900 CE. The Dead Sea Scrolls manuscripts were written between 100 BCE and 100 CE. These biblical manuscripts written approximately 900 years prior were virtually identical to the texts from 900 CE.[10] This practice of meticulous copying was undoubtedly transferred to the early copying of New Covenant documents.

Additionally, scholars have discovered 5,838 portions of the New Covenant written in Greek, 25,000 ancient manuscripts of New Covenant writings in other languages, and over 1,000,000 quotations from early church father writings quoting the New Covenant.[11] The more copies of an ancient document available, the more difficult the copies would have been to alter. The sheer number of virtually identical "pieces" to this puzzle that have been discovered has essentially nullified any variances found within the ancient documents. In fact, although no original texts of the books and letters in the New Covenant have been discovered, historians estimate that we can know with 99.5% certainty what was written in the original documents by comparing these numerous manuscripts.[12]

If any non-biblical text were written over 2,000 years ago and held 99.5% textual certainty, it would be truly amazing. Dr. John Warwick Montgomery explains:

> To be skeptical of the resultant text of the New Testament books is to allow all of classical antiquity to slip into

obscurity, for no documents of the ancient period are as well attested bibliographically as the New Testament.[13]

By comparison, there remain only 210 copies of Plato's famous writings about the teachings of Socrates written in their original language, and no credible source doubts their accuracy.[14] The fact that there are remarkably fewer copies of Socrates teachings does not deem them to be historically inaccurate, but it does lead us to conclude that we can view the texts of the New Covenant, including the gospels, as having a higher degree of textual certainty.

Claim 2: There are too Many Contradictions

Another common argument among individuals attempting to render the gospels as inaccurate historical documents is that they are perceived as being contradictory in places. I also have initially thought some passages were inconsistent only to later realize I had jumped to a conclusion and was mistaken. My mistakes were often because I read a section out of context, did not understand the culture at the time, or did not consider the perspective of the author.

One example of these seemingly contradictory accounts of some of the details of the resurrection in the gospels is the difference in how many angels appeared to the women to proclaim the resurrection of Yeshua. The Gospel of Matthew discusses the *activity* of one angel,[15] but the Gospel of John mentions the *presence* of two angels.[16] These accounts are not contradictory. Matthew does not exclude the existence of another angel when he describes the activity of one angel. A radio announcer may describe the activities of a running back on the football field, but that does not exclude the other 21 players involved in the play on the field at that time. It merely means the focus was on the running back during that particular play. Perceived discrepancies in the gospels, such as the number of angels who appeared to the women the morning of the resurrection, do not render the entire narrative inaccurate.

Imagine that a group of college students visit the famous Louvre Art Museum in Paris, France. Each will have a slightly different perspective and story to tell of their visit. Some may describe how crowded all the rooms were. Others may say nothing about the crowds, but will focus on the beauty of the artwork. Would these different accounts make every testimony inaccurate? Of course not! We would surmise the stories varied slightly because of the different perspective of the individual sharing the narrative. In a court of law, if testimony offered from two witnesses is the exact same, it is often argued that since different witnesses virtually never see matters exactly the same, the identical stories were rehearsed in an effort to deceive. Thus, the different perspectives of each gospel narrative actually increase their historicity because these differences indicate that there was no orchestrated effort to deceive.

As with the group of college students visiting the Louvre, every writer had different perspectives from which they based their narrative about Yeshua. To help illustrate this point further, I identify as a father, husband, son, brother, uncle, lawyer, and author. If someone says that I am an author, someone who only knows me as a lawyer may disagree. Although their description is an incomplete assessment, it is not inaccurate. We cannot expect every piece of historical evidence to encompass the entirety of a historical event. In the same way, we cannot expect each gospel to narrate identical details of Yeshua's life and resurrection. However, by looking at the gospels in their entirety, along with other sources, we are able to piece together a more complete description of the life, death, and resurrection of Yeshua.[17]

Claim 3: There is No Non-Biblical Evidence

Josephus: Affirms Execution of John the Baptist

It is significant that the historical accuracy of the Bible is also confirmed by non-Biblical ancient sources. Flavius Josephus is one of the most well-known ancient Roman historians. He was born to a highly respected Jewish priest in Jerusalem in 37 CE, only a few years after the crucifixion of Yeshua. Jewish customs, practices, and beliefs were ingrained in Josephus throughout much of his life. He eventually joined the Romans as a historian for the Emperor Vespasian.[18] It was at the urging of the Jewish leadership that the Romans crucified Yeshua, so they clearly had no motive to perpetuate the gospel narratives if they were not true. Josephus records that John the Baptist, a first century Jewish prophet, was killed at the direction of Herod. This aligns with the gospel accounts of the death of John the Baptist. Josephus wrote in approximately 90 CE, "And so John, out of Herod's suspiciousness, was sent in chains to Machaerus, the fort previously mentioned, and there put to death."[19]

The Gospel of Mark records the same event: "Immediately the king (Herod) sent an executioner and commanded his (John the Baptist's) head to be brought. And he went and beheaded him in prison," (parentheticals added), (Mark 6:27).[20]

Josephus: Identifies James as Yeshua's Brother

Josephus also identified James as the brother of Yeshua, which the gospels described. Josephus writes, "He brought before them the brother of Jesus who was called Christ, whose name was James."[21] This is confirmed in the Gospel of Mark which also notes how those who had watched Yeshua grow up were amazed at his "wisdom" and "mighty works."

Many hearing Him were astonished, saying, "Where did this man get these things? And what wisdom is that which is given to Him, that such mighty works are performed by his hands! Is this not the carpenter, the Son of Mary, and *brother of James*?" (emphasis added), (Mark 6:2-3).[22]

Roman Official: Pontius Pilate

Because of its theological significance and life changing ramifications, the Bible, more than most other historical documents, has been extensively scrutinized for any statements that may be found to be historically inaccurate. History takes time to uncover, but as more discoveries have been made, the validity of the Bible is continually confirmed. Biblical stories that have wrongly been accused of being stories of folklore have been confirmed by archeological discoveries. For instance, the gospels record that Pontius Pilate was the Roman Official of Judea during the life of Yeshua.[23] Along with references to Pilate in the ancient writings of historians Tacitus[24] and Josephus,[25] [26] archeologists have discovered a stone near Jerusalem inscribed with the name of Pilate during that period. This indicates that there was a Roman official with the name of "Pilate" during the crucifixion of Yeshua, just as the gospels record.[27]

Remains of Crucified Body Discovered

Another significant archaeological discovery verifies the details of the crucifixion of Yeshua. Some had claimed that the gospel narrative of the crucifixion could not have been true because it was not common practice in the Roman Empire to bury their crucified victims. (The gospels record that Yeshua was buried in a tomb after His crucifixion.) However, archeologists have discovered the buried remains of a man crucified at the hands of the Romans, confirming that Yeshua could have been placed in a tomb after His crucifixion, just as the gospels record.[28]

Legacy of Yeshua

Again, comparing the historical evidence for Yeshua to the historical evidence for Alexander the Great demonstrates the unwarranted bias against historical evidence when dealing with biblical figures, especially Yeshua. Apart from the five sources of written evidence often used to prove the life of Alexander the Great (discussed previously), individuals also use the cities and legacy he left as proof of his existence. This same logic could be used for Yeshua (albeit, it is not great historical logic, but helps demonstrate the reality of the prejudice nonetheless). Yeshua has a following that has been in existence for 2,000 years. The following of Yeshua has been in effect far longer than that of Alexander the Great. So it is extremely biased to use "city" legacy of Alexander the Great as proof of his existence, and not use the lasting legacy of Yeshua.

* *

Prolific New Covenant scholar F.F. Bruce felt the major stumbling block for biblical skeptics came from their personal religious beliefs, not the historicity of the Bible. He concludes, "If the New Testament were a collection of secular writings, their authenticity would generally be regarded as beyond all doubt."[29] If historians often use ancient documents written by first and second-hand witnesses as evidence to prove a historical event, why would we ignore four writings fulfilling these credentials? Is it because of the lack of historical evidence to support the gospels, or because of ones religious beliefs?

For the duration of this discussion, emphasis will be placed on non-biblical sources when available. However, New Covenant texts will also be used as they too offer historical evidence. It is illogical to assume the gospels cannot be utilized as historical evidence simply because they are a part of what some regard to be a sacred writing. Although many scholars do not believe in the divine inspiration of the text, they accept the gospels for what they are—historical accounts written within 35-70 years of the death of Yeshua.

I encourage you to set aside your beliefs about whether the Bible is divinely inspired, and scrutinize the evidence presented as if you were researching the life of any other individual in history.

DID YESHUA LIVE AND DIE IN ISRAEL 2,000 YEARS AGO?

One of the most important means of determining the validity of a historical event is the examination of a testimony from someone who disagrees with your conclusion. In a court of law that is referred to as testimony from a hostile or "adverse witness." Any testimony from an adverse witness even slightly favorable to your position is considered persuasive, as such a witness is certainly not going to lie or exaggerate to help your case.

For example, if the mother of a man charged with murder testifies that her son left home angry on the day of the murder and almost always carried a handgun, her testimony is extremely beneficial to the prosecution's case. Her testimony is helpful even if she also testifies that her son was headed to his friend's house, which is in the opposite direction of the crime scene (so he could not be responsible). The prosecutor would point out the reliability of the portion of the mother's testimony in which she acknowledges her son left home angry, and probably had a handgun the night of the murder. As an adverse witness to the prosecution, she would certainly not lie about those facts to help the prosecution.

When I was a young attorney and preparing for one of my first trials, I called my older brother for advice. He is a more experienced attorney, and is now a judge. He shared how he often likes to call an adverse witness as his first witness. This demonstrates how even the opposition agrees with certain key points of his case. I am going to follow my brother's suggestion. Compiled in the following section are three of the many testimonies from individuals who lived around the time of Yeshua, but did not believe Yeshua is the

Messiah, thereby making them adverse witnesses to the followers of Yeshua.[30] Nonetheless, they provide statements that Yeshua lived and died at the hands of the Romans, just as the gospels record.

Adverse Witness 1: Josephus

The ancient historian Josephus also recorded in his writing *Antiquities of the Jews* that Yeshua lived, was a "doer of startling deeds," and was executed on a cross. In this book, Josephus also seems to hold Yeshua in high esteem and did not consider him to be either a lunatic or deceiver:

> At that time there appeared Jesus, a wise man. For he was a doer of startling deeds, a teacher of people who receive the truth with pleasure. And he gained a following both among many Jews and among many of Greek origin. And when Pilate [a Roman], because of an accusation made by leading men among us [the Jews], condemned him to the cross, those who had loved him previously did not cease to do so. And up until this very day the tribe of Christians [named after him] has not died out.[31]

As is written by Josephus, the Gospel of Matthew also records that Yeshua lived and was condemned to die at the insistence of the Jewish religious leaders at the time. While on trial with the high priest, Yeshua was asked whether He was the Son of God. Yeshua responded, "You have said so," (Matthew 26:64).[32] After Yeshua's response, the Jewish Sanhedrin claimed Yeshua deserved death for speaking blasphemy against God:

> Then the high priest tore his clothes saying, "He has spoken blasphemy! What further need do we have of

witnesses? Look, now you have heard His blasphemy! What do you think?" They answered and said, "He is deserving of death," (Matthew 26:63-66).[33]

As this passage from the Gospel of Matthew demonstrates, the Pharisees despised the message that Yeshua preached. What motive does Josephus, a Jewish man writing for the Romans, have to fabricate the existence, "startling deeds," and execution of Yeshua? None!

Adverse Witness 2: The Babylonian Talmud

A second source affirming the life and death of Yeshua comes from the Jewish Babylonian Talmud, a foundational text in Judaism written by rabbinic leaders who did not follow Yeshua. In these writings, the rabbis also provide an account of the crucifixion of Yeshua (whom they call Yeshu, which is a derogatory term often used to describe Yeshua). Their account of the crucifixion of Yeshua is consistent with the narrative in the gospel writings that also place Yeshua's death on the eve of Passover. The Gospel of John records:

> Since it was the day of Preparation (for Passover), and so that the bodies would not remain on the cross on the Sabbath [for that Sabbath was a high day], the Jews asked Pilate that their legs might be broken and that they might be taken away, (parenthetical added), (John 19:31).[34]

The Babylonian Talmud also confirms that Yeshua was crucified on the eve of Passover just at the gospels record.

> It has been taught: On the Eve of the Passover, they hanged Yeshu. And an announcer went out in front of him, for forty days saying: "He is going to be stoned

because he practiced sorcery and enticed and led Israel astray. Anyone who knows anything in his favor, let him come and plead on his behalf." But, not having found anything in his favor, they hanged him on the Eve of Passover.[35]

During this time, "hanged" was synonymous with crucifixion, (when someone is hung on a cross). The same term is used in the New Covenant:

The Messiah (Yeshua) redeemed us from the curse pronounced in the *Torah* by becoming cursed on our behalf; for the Tanakh (Old Covenant) says, "Everyone who *hangs* from a stake comes under a curse," (parentheticals and emphasis added), (Galatians 3:13).[36]

These rabbis believed Yeshua was blaspheming against God. As such, they would have desired this movement be dissolved and forgotten as quickly as possible. There is no motive for prominent rabbis to record in the Babylonian Talmud this depiction of the life and death of Yeshua on the eve of Passover, just as the New Covenant notes. Why would they record facts confirming the New Covenant account of the life and death of a man whom they despised, *unless* the facts they wrote were true? They wouldn't. Clearly, Yeshua lived and was crucified on the eve of Passover, as confirmed by the Babylonian Talmud.

Similarly, Maimonides (Rambam) is a very highly regarded 12th century rabbi and scholar. He wrote a 14-volume work called the Mishne Torah in which he made multiple references to Yeshua and his execution. He writes, "Jesus of Nazareth who aspired to be the Messiah and was executed by the court."[37] Maimonides, although not a follower of Yeshua, also acknowledged Yeshua truly lived and was executed.

Adverse Witness 3: Tacitus

The Annals, written by Roman senator Tacitus in 115 CE, provides a third confirmation from an adverse witness to the life and crucifixion of Yeshua. Tacitus was a Roman Senator during the time of active Roman persecution of Christians. *The Annals* reiterates the New Covenant account that Pontius Pilate executed a man named "Christ," and tortured His followers who were known as "Christians:"

> Therefore, to squelch the rumor, Nero created scapegoats and subjected to the most refined tortures those whom the common people called "Christians," [a group] hated for their abominable crimes. Their name comes from Christ, who, during the reign of Tiberius, *had been executed* by the procurator Pontius Pilate. Suppressed for the moment, the deadly superstition broke out again, not only in Judea, the land which originated this evil, but also in the city of Rome, (emphasis added).[38]

Some have argued that because crucifixion was a common practice throughout the Roman Empire, there may have been another man executed by Pontius Pilate also named "Christ," (which means Messiah), to whom this quote refers. This argument is without merit because, as noted in the above excerpt, Tacitus' writings also describe the "most refined torture" and execution inflicted on those who claimed that Yeshua was the Messiah ("common people called 'Christians.'") Thus, Tacitus clearly connects the above passages to Yeshua and His followers. If the existence and execution of Yeshua were truly a hoax, why would Tacitus record a lie to support the beliefs of a group of people he probably despised?

LIAR, LUNATIC, OR LORD?

Good documentation, especially from reliable witnesses, will usually make or break a case. All of the previous witnesses are reliable historical witnesses because, despite being opposed to Yeshua and His followers, they confirm the gospel accounts of His life and death. Individuals who did not have an ulterior motive to perpetuate any lies about the life of Yeshua penned these three historical documents relatively near the time of His life and death. These texts, along with many others, provide compelling evidence leading historians to conclude that Yeshua's life and eventual crucifixion by Pontius Pilate are true historical events, just as the gospels record.

Most who have a problem with Yeshua are not concerned with whether He lived, or even whether He prompted an impressive and long-lasting following. In fact, most who do not believe in the divinity of Yeshua may still claim that He was a wonderful teacher.[39] However, the declarations Yeshua made during His ministry do not allow for such a neutral perspective. Yeshua claimed that He was God in the flesh[40] and had the power to forgive sins.[41] These statements (along with others made by Yeshua) led the Jewish Sanhedrin (the highest council of the Jewish people at the time) to demand His execution. These statements also led C.S. Lewis to conclude in his highly acclaimed book *Mere Christianity*, that if Yeshua made such claims, He must either be a liar, a lunatic, or who He said He was, LORD.[42][43] The historical evidence is stacked against Yeshua being either a liar or lunatic. Notably, most rabbis and Jewish leaders today acknowledge that Yeshua was neither a liar nor lunatic and He is considered to have been a brilliant rabbi and a righteous man.[44]

Can we truly conclude that He is LORD? With the billions of people who have lived over the course of human history some (albeit, not many), have spurred new religious followings. Most are not bothered by the life of Yeshua, or even His polarizing claims. What truly bothers some is who people claim He is—God in the flesh. It is historically undeniable that Yeshua lived and was executed at the hands of the Romans. His followers believe He died for the sins of the world, was resurrected from the dead, and is now seated in heaven at the right hand of the Father as the Son of God and prophesied Messiah of Israel. Despite how outlandish these claims may seem, as we will explore in the next section, the resurrection of Yeshua is also a remarkably well-documented historical event.

WAS YESHUA RESURRECTED FROM THE DEAD?

Despite all of the evidence supporting the resurrection, one question remains. How did this seemingly impossible event occur? We struggle to wrap our minds around this, and justifiably so. We are faced with a daunting paradox: can a historic event be validated despite its miraculous nature?

Some may argue that although miracles were considered a possibility in ancient times, we now understand that they defy the laws of science. However, even in ancient times, someone being raised from the dead was astonishing and unexpected. In fact, it is recorded in the Gospel of Matthew that when some of the disciples saw Yeshua resurrected, they too doubted.[45] These were the men Yeshua had spent much of the previous three years with, and yet some did not believe He had been truly resurrected from the dead. If resurrections were extremely common and believable in ancient times, why would some of the disciples have initially doubted? It is significant that these same disciples were later willing to be tortured and brutally killed for their belief in the resurrected Yeshua, so obviously their doubts were completely eliminated.

One of the leading arguments against the historicity of the resurrection is the belief that all events that may seem supernatural actually have natural explanations. However, as Timothy Keller illuminates in his New York Times best-selling book *The Reason for God*, this non-acceptance of the supernatural is also rooted in faith. He writes, "It is one thing to say that science is only equipped to test for natural causes and cannot speak to any others. It is quite another to insist that science proves that no other causes could possibly exist."[46] To believe only in science is itself an act of faith. To say that nothing in life can occur without a scientific explanation is no longer a statement of science, but is one with philosophical assumptions behind it.[47]

Similarly, the belief there are no miracles and the supernatural realm cannot exist is completely extinguished if there is a creator of the universe. It stands to reason that if there is a God or a higher power (as—90% of American's believe to be the case, according to a recent Pew Research Center survey)[48] then He could easily surpass the laws of physics making miracles a possibility. Understandably, we should not immediately conclude an event that seems miraculous is in fact a miracle. We should have a critical eye, as many "miraculous events" have been determined to be false.[49] But, to completely write off the possibility of a miraculous explanation is to sorely limit our ability to understand what has truly occurred.

Perhaps you do not currently believe in miracles. I would challenge you to continue to read on as we examine the historical evidence for the resurrection of Yeshua. If the evidence is convincing, should we ignore the possibility of a miraculous event? I believe it will become clear that Yeshua not only lived and was crucified, but despite its miraculous nature, was also resurrected from the dead.

ANCIENT REFERENCES TO YESHUA'S MIRACLES

Yeshua was not a normal man. As the renowned and highly esteemed Rabbi Maimonides, the respected Roman historian Josephus, the gospel writers, and others describe, Yeshua performed miracles everywhere He went. Many of these miracles were witnessed by hundreds of people. As noted above, Josephus referred to Yeshua as "a doer of startling deeds," which is a similar description he used in referencing the miracles of the Jewish prophet Elisha.[50] [51]

Similarly, the second century Roman author Celsus wrote *The True Word,* which was a critique of those following Yeshua.[52] He believed faith in Yeshua was interfering with individuals' allegiance to Rome. Celsus writes this concerning the miracles and life of Yeshua:

> That he (Jesus)... coming to the knowledge of certain *miraculous power,* returned from thence to his own country, and by means of those powers proclaimed himself a god, (parenthetical and emphasis added).[53]

Celsus was also an adverse witness and despised the followers of Yeshua—he wrote an entire book about why he felt they were crazy![54] So he clearly had no reason to lie and concede that Yeshua was a miraculous man who had supernatural powers.

The Babylonian Talmud also refers to the supernatural and miraculous nature of the life of Yeshua. It says in *Sanhedrin 43a*:

> On the Eve of the Passover, they hanged Yeshu. And an announcer went out in front of him, for forty days saying: "He is going to be stoned because he *practiced sorcery* and enticed and led Israel astray," (emphasis added).[55]

The writers of these rabbinic commentaries clearly refer to Yeshua practicing "sorcery," which means that He was performing acts that were perceived as being miraculous. Although these writers probably did not regard Yeshua as LORD, they clearly refer to His life as miraculous.

Respected and credentialed biblical theologian Dr. John Meier surmises that in light of the vast amount of documentation of Yeshua's miracles, it would be virtually impossible for them to have been fabricated:

> The miracle traditions about Jesus' public ministry are already so widely attested in various sources and literary forms by the end of the first Christian generation that total fabrication by the early church is, practically speaking, impossible.[56]

The life of Yeshua was clearly perceived as being miraculous. As Yeshua lived a life filled with seemingly supernatural events, it does not seem preposterous to presume another major miraculous event (His resurrection) could have occurred.

THE EVIDENCE FOR THE RESURRECTION

Miracles performed by Yeshua establish a foundation upon which the resurrection can be built; but the ultimate issue is the resurrection itself. As we have seen, historians often draw their conclusions based upon facts that are virtually uncontroverted. In other words, historians determine the explanations for *why* events occurred from the available evidence. Utilizing this method, historians have determined that four compelling facts exist which strongly supports the resurrection. These facts will be referred to as "Exhibits." Each exhibit alone may not convince you of the resurrection of Yeshua. However, any hypothesis denying the resurrection must offer a compelling explanation that addresses *all* four exhibits.

After examining the historical facts for the resurrection of Yeshua, we will then analyze the common alternative theories and explanations offered for the evidence presented—other than the resurrection. For instance, our first "Exhibit" (the empty tomb) is an essentially uncontroverted historical fact. The sealed and guarded tomb in which Yeshua was laid was later found to be empty. However, some have different theories as to *why* His tomb was empty (other than the resurrection of Yeshua). After this examination of the rebuttal theories, I believe you will then be in a position to render a verdict either for, or against, the resurrection of Yeshua. We will start by exploring the evidence of:

Exhibit A: The Empty Tomb
Exhibit B: Witnesses to the Resurrected Yeshua
Exhibit C: The Commitment of the Disciples of
              Yeshua Amidst Adverse Circumstances
Exhibit D: Silence From the Opposition

Exhibit A: The Empty Tomb

After Yeshua was crucified, His followers dispersed. They returned to their old jobs and denied their association with Him.[57] That is, until they discovered that His tomb was empty three days later. As Josephus noted, the following of Yeshua "did not die out" after His death.[58] In fact, it grew rapidly. The momentum of His following would have been abruptly halted if the corpse of Yeshua was discovered, or if there was evidence of foul play. Paul Althaus, a professor of practical and systematic theology at the University of Göttingen, reasons:

> (The resurrection) could have not been maintained in Jerusalem for a single day, for a single hour, if the emptiness of the tomb had not been established as an undeniable fact for all concerned, (parenthetical added).[59]

Yet, there is no evidence that the corpse of Yeshua has ever been discovered. It seems clear that the tomb in which the body of

Yeshua was laid after the crucifixion was empty, corroborating the testimonies of eyewitnesses claiming they had seen the resurrected Yeshua.

N. T. Wright, an eminent British New Covenant scholar, concludes, "That is why, as an historian, I cannot explain the rise of early Christianity unless Jesus rose again, leaving an empty tomb behind him."[60]

The Romans despised anything other than allegiance to Rome. The Jewish religious leaders believed Yeshua was blaspheming by claiming that He was the Son of God.[61] They brought Him to Pontius Pilate who ordered the crucifixion of Yeshua.[62] He was a high profile political prisoner who was causing quite a disturbance. The Roman and Jewish leaders would have jumped on any opportunity to demonstrate the illegitimacy of the resurrection of Yeshua, and one foolproof way to accomplish this would have been to simply produce His corpse once word of the resurrection began to spread. Any uprising would have been immediately squelched if the corpse of Yeshua were displayed in a public area. After studying the barbaric nature of a Roman Crucifixion, displaying Yeshua's body for all to see seems like a quick and easy solution to the problem presented.[63]

As there is no evidence that either the Jewish or Roman leaders revealed the corpse of Yeshua, it seems at least plausible that the tomb was, in fact, empty. The Book of Acts, which is a historical documentation of the beginning of the following of Yeshua, mentions the empty tomb. Amazingly, the main debate in Acts is *why* the tomb was empty, not *if* it was empty.[64] No need existed for the disciples to make a major issue of the emptiness of the tomb. Anyone who was skeptical of the empty tomb could have simply gone to look. If they would have found the body of Yeshua still in the tomb, they could have displayed His corpse for everyone to see. If His tomb were not empty, it would have been an easily verifiable fact that surely would have been documented by either the Jewish or Roman leadership in order to extinguish the uprising.

Some may speculate that the verification could not have been so simple because travel in ancient times was much more difficult. They may presume, perhaps people were more akin to believing in things that did not happen because they could not actually go and see it for themselves. Although travel was obviously more difficult in ancient times than it is now, the following of Yeshua began in the *Pax Romana,* a time when the Roman civilization was relatively at peace, and there were many accomplishments and advances throughout the empire. Most notably to our discussion, the Romans built an extensive roadway system, which would have made travel much easier.[65] Also, Yeshua's tomb was within walking distance in Jerusalem, making it easily accessible for any skeptics who did not believe it was empty.

The story of the resurrected Yeshua would never have circulated so widely without the validation of an empty tomb by eyewitnesses. As the empty tomb seems to be an undisputed fact, this has led to three major theories offered by skeptics to explain why the tomb of Yeshua was empty aside from His resurrection:

Theory 1: The Body of Yeshua was Stolen
Theory 2: Everyone Looked for Yeshua in the Wrong Tomb
Theory 3: Yeshua was Never Killed During His Crucifixion

Theory 1: The Body of Yeshua Was Stolen

Response: Yeshua's followers had no access to the tomb, and His enemies had no motive to remove His body.

The most circulated explanation as to why the tomb was empty is that the disciples stole the body of Yeshua. Even the Gospel of Matthew relays that this is a speculation as old as the resurrection.

> While they were going, behold, some of the guard came into the city and reported to the chief priests all the things that had happened. When they had assembled with the elders and consulted together, they gave a large sum of money to the soldiers saying, "Tell them, 'His disciples came at night and stole Him away while we slept.' And if this comes to the governor's ears, we will appease him and make you secure." So they took the money and did as they were instructed; and this saying is commonly reported among the Jews until this day, (Matthew 28:11-15).[66]

Just a reminder, if you are rolling your eyes and thinking that the gospels cannot be used as a historical source, please review the section above confirming their historical value. Although the gospels have not been used exclusively as historical evidence, since they were written within the time frame of 35-70 years after Yeshua's crucifixion, categorically rejecting them seems illogical. As previously noted, any historical evidence written this close to an event during this time in antiquity is deemed extremely reliable.

According to this verse, the Roman guards immediately began the narrative of a con job devised by the disciples. This is significant because it demonstrates that the Jewish leaders did not deny the tomb was empty. Instead, they provided an unsubstantiated theory to *explain* the empty tomb. A major problem with this theory is that those who were motivated to steal the body of Yeshua had no access to the tomb. Again, if there were *any* proof that the disciples stole the body of Yeshua, the Roman and Jewish leaders would have brought it forth in an attempt to invalidate the narrative being told by Yeshua's close followers, as well as the hundreds of eyewitness who were claiming that Yeshua was resurrected from the dead.

The Roman guards had access to the tomb of Yeshua. However, Roman soldiers were extremely loyal, if not by choice, then out of self-preservation. Under Roman law, the only people who could be subjected to the torturous execution of a crucifixion were non-Roman criminals and *disobedient Roman soldiers*. The soldiers guarding Yeshua's tomb would have understood the serious repercussions of abandoning their post, or of allowing someone to steal the corpse of a prisoner. They too could be crucified.[67] George Currie, a scholar of ancient Roman military describes, "The punishment for abandoning your military post was death, according to the laws."[68] Upholding their post (and guarding the tomb) was quite literally a life or death situation, and these trained guards would not have been careless enough to fall asleep or wander off. The Roman Empire chose topnotch guards and not a Barney Fife or Chief Wiggum type.[69]

The Roman Empire thrived because of its persistence in ensuring no allegiance was sworn to anyone but Rome. Yeshua came preaching a very different message. He continually referred to the Kingdom of God, calling people to "Seek first the Kingdom of God and His righteousness," (Matthew 6:33).[70] The Roman leaders undoubtedly despised this message. The motto of the Roman Empire was to seek first the Kingdom of Rome, and maintain allegiance only to Rome. Further, although the Romans were not yet actively persecuting the followers of Yeshua at this time, they would not have wanted their brutal crucifixion process undermined by the claim that a Jewish peasant carpenter had lived through their most intense form of torture and capital punishment.

After the crucifixion of Yeshua, the Pharisees approached Pontius Pilate to remind him that Yeshua claimed that He would defeat death after three days.[71] The Pharisees requested that all precautions be put into place for Yeshua's tomb. Pilate gave them permission to "Make the tomb secure, seal the stone, and set the guard as best they knew how," (Matthew 27:65-66).[72]

Again, non-biblical sources (noted previously) thoroughly document that the Jewish religious leaders despised Yeshua and His teachings. They wanted Yeshua to be punished for His blasphemy. Clearly, they would have done everything to make Yeshua's tomb as secure as they could so as not to condone what they believed to be a lie against God. As the Gospel of Mark records, the entrance to the tomb of Yeshua was secured with a large stone:

> When the Sabbath was past, Mary Magdalene, Mary the mother of James, and Salome bought spices so they might come and anoint Him. Very early in the morning, on the first day of the week, they came to the tomb when the sun had risen. And they said among themselves, "Who will roll away the stone from the door of the tomb for us?" But when they looked up, they saw that the stone had been rolled away—it was very large, (Mark 16:1-4).[73]

Although I'm sure these women who lived in an extremely patriarchal society were not exactly body builders, we can imagine that the stone blocking the entrance was extremely large if all three of them thought they could not move it together. The stone was also "sealed" to prevent individuals from breaking in. The early 20th century New Covenant scholar A. T. Robertson describes the probable process of sealing the tomb. Robertson explains that the Romans likely stretched a cord across the stone covering the entrance to the tomb, and then placed a Roman Seal on either end of the cord.[74] Before placing the seal, the Romans would have ensured the tomb was secured and inescapable. The Roman Seal was held with high regard, and the punishment inflicted upon someone who broke the seal would have been severe.

To summarize, the historical evidence simply does not support the theory that the body of Yeshua was stolen. His followers had no access to his tomb, and His enemies had no reason to steal His body. The Jewish leaders demanded that Yeshua be executed for His blasphemy against God, and because of their influence over the Roman Governor Pontius Pilate, the Romans then executed Yeshua. Although historically Rome was not actively persecuting followers of Yeshua at this time, its leaders still would have not wanted their highest form of torture and death to be undermined; thus, Yeshua's tomb was surrounded by intense security. Highly loyal and skilled Roman soldiers guarded the tomb, and a large heavy stone was placed in front of the entrance and was then secured by the Roman Seal. Professor D.H. Van Daalen offers up his own sentiments for the reason some adhere to the stolen body theory:

> It is extremely difficult to object to the empty tomb on historical grounds; those who deny it do so on the basis of theological or philosophical assumptions.[75]

Theory 2: Everyone Looked for Yeshua in the Wrong Tomb

Response: It was only a three-day time span between Yeshua's burial and resurrection, so it seems implausible that all of His followers and enemies would have forgotten where He was buried.

Some have argued that Yeshua was simply not in the tomb where everyone was looking. They propose that everyone was confused about where Yeshua was buried because the tombs all looked similar. This hypothesis was never even proposed until 1907 by Kirsopp Lake, and it seems to be nothing more than wishful thinking.[76]

It seems unlikely that *everyone* in Jerusalem would have forgotten where this high profile prisoner was placed. Also, it is recorded that the tomb belonged to Joseph of Arimathea who asked Pilate for Yeshua's body so he could give Him a proper burial.[77] If Joseph were the owner of the tomb, he would have known where it was. If the tomb did not belong to Joseph, he still would have known the location because he had performed Yeshua's burial only three days prior.

Even if Joseph had forgotten which tomb Yeshua was laid in, Mary Magdalene was also a witness to Yeshua's crucifixion and resurrection.[78] It is recorded that she was at the burial of Yeshua, and was one of the women who went to bring spices to anoint His body only to find His tomb empty.[79] She probably would not have forgotten where the man she regarded as her LORD had been buried only three days prior.

If you do not believe the biblical accounts, think about the highly motivated individuals who were trying to stop this new world-changing movement. Once people began to claim Yeshua was resurrected from the dead, the Jewish or Roman leaders could have easily gone to the correct tomb and presented Yeshua's body. Undoubtedly, the Romans, who would have not wanted their brutal execution process undermined, would have displayed Yeshua's body in a grotesque and public manner. Had this been done, belief in Yeshua would have been immediately extinguished. Instead, the inability of the Jewish and Roman leadership to produce a corpse or a credible explanation for the empty tomb is quite possibly the best evidence that the body of Yeshua was not laying in another tomb. Again, this "wrong tomb" theory is unsupported by the historical evidence.

Theory 3: Yeshua Was Never Killed During His Crucifixion

Response: Crucifixions were absolutely brutal. Yeshua would have had to make a miraculous escape after this punishment, and then He would have had to be deemed fully healed by His followers three days later.

Some accept that the tomb was empty, but do not believe that Yeshua was ever truly dead. They believe that Yeshua fell unconscious (or swooned), and was never actually killed during the crucifixion. They believe after He regained consciousness, He simply snuck out of the tomb. While Yeshua was still hanging on His execution stake, Pilate wanted to confirm that Yeshua was truly dead.[80] Pilate asked his centurion (a Roman military officer) to verify the death of Yeshua. The Romans were well accustomed to death, as crucifixions and executions were common practice throughout the empire. They would have known what a post-mortem individual looked like.

After Pilate was assured that Yeshua was dead, Joseph of Arimathea prepared the body of Yeshua for burial. Jewish custom required the body be washed, "Then bandaged tightly from the armpits to the ankles in strips of linen about a foot wide."[81] The Gospel of John confirms this custom was followed.[82] If Yeshua had awoken, He would have had to unwrap his tight whole-body cast, move the large stone sealing the entrance to the tomb, break the Roman Seal, and sneak out past a heavily guarded entrance.

This would have been a nearly impossible feat for anyone to accomplish, even if someone were in a state of perfect health. Let's remember even skeptics of the resurrection confirm that Yeshua was severely beaten, tortured, and left to die while nailed to a cross by his hands and feet, (refer to Tacitus' quote). To confirm Yeshua's death, one of the centurions plunged a spear into Yeshua's right side, likely puncturing a lung or one of his vital organs.[83]

Now try to imagine a man who would have been in that kind of condition waking up, only to execute a James Bond-esque escape under the noses of the brutal Roman guards. After His miraculous escape, His extensive wounds would have to be significantly healed in three days in order to persuade hundreds of people who saw Him that He was fully recovered and resurrected from the dead.

Perhaps the most compelling evidence that Yeshua died by crucifixion comes from an in-depth review of the crucifixion of Yeshua, published by the esteemed *Journal of the American Medical Association*. This article verifies that Yeshua died on His execution stake. After reviewing the evidence, the article concludes, "Interpretations based on the assumption that Jesus did not die on the cross appear to be at odds with modern medical knowledge."[84] It seems as if the "swoon theory" may take more faith to believe in than the resurrection.

* *

There has yet to be a logical substantiated explanation for the empty tomb of Yeshua, aside from His resurrection. If we choose to deny the resurrection, we are left with the unsolved mystery of why His tomb was empty. If Yeshua's empty tomb were the only evidence historians could use to validate His resurrection, it would be a convincing case. However, there are still three more historical facts we have yet to explore: the witnesses to the resurrected Yeshua, the commitment of Yeshua's disciples despite severe repercussions, and the lack of evidence from the opposing side.

Exhibit B: Witnesses to the Resurrected Yeshua

Now we are left with this question: if Yeshua was miraculously resurrected from the tomb, where did He go and what did He do? One of the best sources of witnesses of the resurrected Yeshua comes from the first letter to the Corinth Church ("1st Corinthians") written by the Apostle Paul (Rabbi Saul of Tarsus) in approximately 55 CE. Paul was a Pharisee (a very strict, observant Jew) who initially rigorously persecuted those who believed Yeshua was the prophesied Messiah.[85] He stood by and approved as Stephen, a follower of Yeshua, was stoned to death for his beliefs.[86]

After a personal supernatural experience on the road to Damascus, Paul immediately became a devoted follower of Yeshua.[87] Paul's transformation from violent persecutor to passionate believer is undeniable. His writings in the New Covenant repeatedly declare his devotion and unwavering commitment to Yeshua.[88]

After his transformation, Paul wrote many letters to the first century churches, some of which are in the New Covenant. In 1st Corinthians, Paul writes, "Then he (Yeshua) appeared to more than five hundred brothers at one time, most of whom are still alive, though some have fallen asleep," (parenthetical added).[89] Paul wrote this passage when most of the 500 witnesses who saw the resurrected Yeshua were still alive![90] If Paul was fibbing or even embellishing, his writings would have been rejected, as there would be no witnesses to support his bold assertions.

Even without Twitter and other social media, the earth-shattering news of a resurrected Messiah would have spread like wildfire. If Paul had lied about the 500 witnesses of the resurrection, there would have been an abundance of people lining up to set the record straight. Remember, travel had become easier during this period in the ancient Roman Empire. Paul even identifies individuals *by name* who saw the resurrected Yeshua.[91] An opponent to Yeshua could have asked any of the witnesses identified whether Paul's claims were true. *One* denier would have been devastating to Paul's written accounts. However, there is *no* evidence of such. If either the Roman or Jewish authorities uncovered evidence of false statements by Paul or *any* of the 500 eyewitnesses, the following of Yeshua would have disbanded.

Lastly, in his writings, Paul acknowledges that he was a "chief persecutor" of the early followers of Yeshua.[92] This does not appear to be something Paul would fabricate about himself if he was trying to join the group he used to persecute. Such an acknowledgement could cause His followers to be quite suspicious of His newfound allegiance and could have caused him to be heavily scrutinized as a possible spy.

His incriminating admission further validates the historical validity of his transforming experience on the road to Damascus.

Since there is little doubt by scholars that individuals believed they had truly seen the risen Yeshua, we will examine one of the more common theories offered to explain why they believed this, other than the resurrection of Yeshua.

The Mass Hallucination Theory

Response: Mass hallucinations provoked by feelings of despair are inconsistent with any psychological findings of how hallucinations operate.

Some have argued that over 500 people *believed* they saw Yeshua, but that it was just a mass hallucination or a vision caused by their immense grief. This theory claims that several hundred people all had similar hallucinations. This is significant for several reasons.

First, hundreds of people would have had to make psychological history and experience the same hallucination at the same time. In other words, this would be the first and only time a mass hallucination has occurred. Clinical psychologist Dr. Gary A. Sibcy points out that even two people experiencing the same hallucination simultaneously has *never* been known to occur:

> I have surveyed the professional literature [peer-reviewed journal articles and books] written by psychologists, psychiatrists, and other relevant healthcare professionals during the past two decades and have yet to find a single documented case of a group hallucination, that is, an event for which more than one person purportedly shared in a visual or other sensory perception where there was clearly no external referent.[93]

It is incredulous to believe that over 500 people experienced the same hallucination of a resurrected Yeshua who was walking, talking, and preaching among them again. According to the gospels, Yeshua made several post-resurrection appearances. They were all visual, auditory, and similarly contextual. It seems illogical to conclude that each of these people experienced such similar hallucinations. If these hundreds of people were so driven to despair by the death of Yeshua that they began hallucinating His resurrection, one would think these personal hallucinations would have varied from individual to individual.

Similarly, this theory does not explain the transformation of Paul. Even if one can overlook the incredible improbability of a mass hallucination, the theory arises from the argument that the hallucination occurred because of immense despair. The transformation of Paul uproots this argument because he was not experiencing despair, yet it is recorded he saw the risen Yeshua. Since he hated Yeshua at the time, this couldn't have come from a feeling of despair.

The belief that hundreds of witnesses hallucinated the same thing at the same time is currently unexplainable and undocumented, making it *extremely* unlikely. Perhaps even more significant, the mass hallucination theory does not even attempt to address why the tomb of Yeshua was empty.

Exhibit C: The Commitment of the Disciples of Yeshua Amidst Adverse Circumstances

The early followers of Yeshua were making a grand historical claim. They were not simply saying that they believed Yeshua was resurrected in the hearts and minds of those who believed in Him. Rather, they were claiming that they had personally interacted with the resurrected Yeshua after He was killed by crucifixion. These early followers were not making these claims based on stories passed down from generation to generation. They were eyewitnesses to the resurrection. Thus, these early followers were either (1) deceived, or (2) attempting to deceive. That is, they all either had the same hallucination of a resurrected Yeshua, or were deliberately spreading a lie.

As we discussed in the previous section, there were over 500 witnesses to the resurrected Yeshua. Despite what some may propose to be an explanation to account for why there is no refutation of these 500 witnesses, we can agree that they were not simultaneously hallucinating the same thing. This leaves the only other option to be that the early followers were attempting to concoct a grandiose lie. As we will see in the following section, because the early followers of Yeshua were facing extremely challenging circumstances, this does not seem like a plausible explanation either.

Adverse Circumstance 1: Terrible Consequences
Adverse Circumstance 2: Unreliable Witnesses
Adverse Circumstance 3: Hard-to-Believe Facts
Adverse Circumstance 4: Illogical Game Plan

Adverse Circumstance 1: Terrible Consequences

These early followers truly believed in what they were preaching. How do we know this? Because they were willing to be imprisoned, tortured, and executed for their cause. Ten of the original twelve disciples were brutally murdered because of their faith in Yeshua. Although people die for false causes all the time, rarely are they willing to be tortured and killed for causes they know to be false because *they made them up*. New Covenant scholar Dr. Michael Licona in his book *The Resurrection of Jesus* describes the commitment of the disciples' beliefs:

> Modern martyrs act solely out of their trust in beliefs passed along to them by others. The apostles died for

holding to their own testimony that they had *personally seen* the risen Jesus…The disciples of Jesus suffered and were willing to die for what they *knew* to be either true or false, (emphasis added).[94]

If the claims of the followers of Yeshua were false, the disciples (Yeshua's closest followers) would have known because they would have been the ones who made it up![95] Yeshua's followers endured horrific torture, such as being boiled in oil and crucified upside-down.[96] This demonstrates their deep conviction and belief that Yeshua's resurrection truly occurred.

Although false prophets and the branching off of new religious sects are fairly common in the 21st century, this would have been blasphemous to Jewish people in ancient Israel. The initial followers of Yeshua were all Jewish. The New Covenant was written entirely by Jews, with the possible exception of the Gospel of Luke and the Book of Acts. These early Jewish believers in Yeshua would have not followed doctrine that they did not truly believe in, as this sort of lie against God could have resulted in harsh consequences.[97]

Even the skeptical German New Covenant scholar Gerd Lüdemann concludes:

It may be taken as *historically certain* that Peter and the disciples had experiences after Jesus' death in which Jesus appeared to them as the risen Christ, (emphasis added).[98]

Now let's turn our attention to the fact that the people telling this story chose poorly constructed ways to do such if they were trying to con individuals into believing something seemingly unbelievable. Rather than choosing a believable "fib," they chose a story laced with unreliable witnesses and hard-to-believe facts. They also chose an extremely illogical game plan to spread their story.

Adverse Circumstance 2: Unreliable Witnesses

What if Yeshua's early followers were trying to sell the most influential and grandiose lie ever told? These early followers were lowly fishermen and tax collectors, not wealthy tycoons or influential people. Even if you do not believe in the deity of Yeshua, the following He inspired has undeniably been one of the most influential movements in the world over the last 2,000 years.[99] The popular historian Will Durant wrote this concerning Yeshua's followers:

> That a few simple men should in one generation have invented so powerful and appealing a personality, so lofty an ethic and so inspiring a vision of human brotherhood, would be a miracle far more incredible than any recorded in the Gospels.[100]

Durant recognizes the unlikelihood of someone choosing the credential-less initial followers of Yeshua if that person were trying to concoct a story. The disciples were not the Bill Gateses, Warren Buffets, or Oprah Winfreys of their day. They were lowly fishermen and tax collectors.[101] Most of these early believers did not have the lofty social status that would be helpful in fabricating an unlikely story.

Adverse Circumstance 3: Hard-to-Believe Facts

Likewise, if the disciples were inventing a story, they were not using very good material. Each gospel writer indicates that Joseph of Arimathea, a prominent man in the Jewish ruling class, performed the burial of Yeshua.[102] A lie about him would have been easy to refute.

The gospels also describe women as the first to discover the empty tomb.[103] At the time, women held no societal power, and any testimony they provided was inadmissible in court.[104] If this truly were a fabricated story, it would have held no credibility. The only way for it to be believable would have been if the women's testimonies were confirmed with physical evidence such as an empty tomb and a multitude of eyewitnesses. If you were going to try to trick people into believing a lie as grandiose as this, it seems you would recruit far better witnesses and develop a far more believable story.

Adverse Circumstance 4: Illogical Game Plan

After the disciples saw the resurrected Yeshua, they did not immediately flee to Athens or Rome to proclaim His resurrection. If they had done so, there would have been no one to refute their testimonies. Although they eventually traveled to spread the news of Yeshua, they initially stayed in Jerusalem where, if they were making everything up, it would have been far easier to discredit their story.[105] Scam artists tend to quickly leave town after they have duped their customers and collected their cash. Yeshua lived, performed many of His miracles, and was crucified in Jerusalem. If the claims of His followers were false and He never lived, performed miraculous acts, and was never resurrected, rebuttal testimonies and evidence would have been readily available. It seems extremely illogical for the disciples to concoct a lie about someone whom many people knew, and then stay in the same location where they were claiming that these events occurred.[106]

Before Yeshua's resurrection, many of His followers denied that they knew Him. Presumably they did such to avoid punishment. When Yeshua was taken in by the Roman guards to be punished and eventually executed, the disciples "forsook Him and fled," (Mark 14:50).[107] Peter, who was one of Yeshua's closest disciples, denied that he knew Yeshua three times.[108]

Yet, when these same disciples later saw Yeshua alive after His crucifixion, they dramatically changed and professed their allegiance to Him, even though it would mean their own torture and death. Peter, the previous denier, preached the divinity of Yeshua to thousands.[109] Quintus Septimius Florens Tertullianus (try saying that three times fast) was a Christian theologian in the early second century. In his writings entitled *Prescription Against Heretics*, he describes the horrific fate of some of the early disciples and followers (Peter, Paul, and John respectively). He affirms:

> How happy is its church, on which apostles poured forth all their doctrine along with their blood! Where Peter endures a passion like his Lord's! Where Paul wins his crown in a death like John's! Where the Apostle John was first plunged, unhurt, into boiling oil, and thence remitted to his island-exile![110]

The followers of Yeshua were not eagerly waiting by the door for Him to rise from the dead. They believed His death by crucifixion was final. Two of the original twelve disciples—Peter and Thomas—returned to their previous occupation of fishermen, essentially believing that the era of Yeshua was over.[111] Clearly, something drastic and miraculous occurred to give these previously downtrodden men something to believe in. As noted above, just before Yeshua's crucifixion, some disciples did not even acknowledge that they knew Him. After Yeshua's resurrection, His followers stood confidently as they were arrested, tortured, and executed for their allegiance and belief in Him. Notable author John R. W. Stott, ranked in 2005 by *Time Magazine* as one of the 100 most influential people in the world, confirms this dramatic change in the lives of the disciples of Yeshua by saying, "Perhaps the transformation of the disciples of Jesus is the greatest evidence of all the resurrection."[112] They changed from cowardly deniers into bold proclaimers.

If the only evidence provided were the unexplainable empty tomb, the case for the resurrection would be compelling. The evidence of the empty tomb coupled with hundreds of witnesses to the resurrected Yeshua plus this radical transformation of the disciples amidst severe persecution have yet to find *any* plausible explanations—other than the reality of the resurrection of Yeshua.

Exhibit D: Silence from the Opposition

In a court of law, if the defense is unable to present *any* compelling evidence refuting the position of the prosecutor, it is an open-and-shut case. As demonstrated, there is overwhelming evidence supporting the life, healing ministry, death, and resurrection of Yeshua. If the Jewish or Roman leaders were able to present *any* evidence calling into question *any* portion of the narrative circulating about Yeshua's life, death, and resurrection, the evidence would have been provided and the following of Yeshua would have been quickly extinguished.[113] In stark contrast, we find many historic writings *supporting* the resurrection of Yeshua as depicted in the narrative of the gospels.

CONCLUSION

After reviewing the historical evidence, the resurrection stands alone as the only plausible explanation. It is not simply the most likely explanation of the evidence; it is the *only* reasonable explanation of the evidence.

Dr. Paul L. Maier is a professor of ancient history and author of both scholarly and public works. He concludes that the evidence for the resurrection supports its historical validity:

> If all the evidence is weighed carefully and fairly, it is indeed justifiable, according to the canons of historical research, to conclude that the sepulcher of Joseph of Arimathea, in which Jesus was buried, was actually empty on the morning of the first Easter. And no shred of evidence has yet been discovered in literary sources, epigraphy, or archaeology that would disprove this statement.[114]

The core of my faith resides in my belief in the resurrection of Yeshua, a supernatural event confirming that He is the promised Messiah and the Son of God.[115] Clearly, there are sources offering opposing theories about what occurred after Yeshua's death and burial. We all must learn to decipher what is truth validated by historical evidence, and what is simply unsubstantiated speculation.

The evidence gathered from adverse ancient witnesses proves Yeshua lived, was crucified, died, and was buried. After Yeshua's crucifixion, His tomb was found empty, hundreds of witnesses claim to have seen Him resurrected, His followers had a drastic change of heart, and His enemies had no verifiable rebuttal. We have uprooted and examined the theories against the resurrection and found them woefully lacking.

As a former Chief Justice in England Lord Charles Darling affirmed, "No intelligent jury in the world could fail to bring in a verdict that the resurrection story is true."[116]

For most of my life, I thought that believing Yeshua lived, was crucified, and was resurrected was simply an idea created in the minds of individuals who needed to feel like there was a greater meaning to life. I thought it was illogical and unsupported by evidence to believe the hype about this one man who *possibly* lived centuries ago. Even after becoming a believer in Yeshua, I assumed believing in His resurrection was based on my faith in Him. This faith was based on the vast impact Yeshua had had on my life. However, after researching the subject for many years, I have discovered there is extremely compelling historical evidence to support His life, crucifixion, and resurrection.

But everything we believe requires some *degree* of faith. Even seemingly rational, modern-day arguments are often rooted in claims based on faith. As was discussed earlier, one of the most common arguments against the resurrection is the idea that we live in a purely natural world, one in which supernatural intervention is an impossibility. This is ultimately based on the faith that we will never find any evidence to the contrary. Clearly, there is convincing evidence supporting the resurrection of Yeshua, despite its miraculous nature. This evidence should not be ignored or taken lightly despite any preconceived notions about miracles.

If you have been convinced, or your curiosity has been even mildly piqued, I invite you to ask Yeshua if He is the promised Messiah of Israel. One night, over 23 years ago, I said I wanted Yeshua in my life—*if* He was real. I silently said a short prayer expressing my desire to know Him. Although there was no burning bush or booming voice from the sky, bit by bit, He broke down barriers I had previously built up against Him and let me know that He is indeed very real. God continues to refine me and speaks into my life daily. I believe if you ask God with an open heart to reveal His Son to you, Yeshua will meet you in the most personal way. And once you meet Him, you will understand the true beauty and love of Yeshua, our Messiah, who is far more than just another historical character.

EPILOGUE

NOW WHAT?

Hopefully you have found the material compiled in this booklet to be helpful in further developing your understanding of God, the Bible, and Yeshua. This information is meant to be a basic foundation, and is by no means comprehensive.[117] As such, I encourage you to continue to research the topics you found interesting. No one will ever discover even a fraction of all there is to know about God.

> Behold, these are but the outskirts of his ways, and how small a whisper do we hear of him! But the thunder of his power who can understand? *Job 26:14* [118]

Often, our minds can be our biggest obstacle in our quest to understand truth. We have certain biases that can be challenging to dislodge. Open your heart and let God know you want to know the truth. If you seek God, you will find Him.

> You will seek me and find me, when you seek me with
> all your heart. *Jeremiah 29:13* [119]

Regardless of whether you are convinced of the resurrection, I encourage you to make a habit of reading the Bible. It will be an invaluable source of insight and wisdom in your life as you grow in your understanding of God. The stories and instructions written in the Bible are not just historically accurate, but are also extremely powerful. They can help to implement change in your life, and the lives of those around you.

> All Scripture is breathed out by God and profitable for
> teaching, for reproof, for correction, and for training in
> righteousness. *2 Timothy 3:16* [120]

However, individual research and learning, even when reading the Bible, will only take you so far *alone*. Finding a community of people earnestly seeking God is vital. Misleading and incorrect information about God and Yeshua is everywhere; having others around to help you discern truth is crucial.

The early followers of Yeshua did life together.[121] They did not simply attend a service one day a week for one hour and expect that they fulfilled their weekly quota of "community time." Even though many of them had lived with Yeshua for three years and saw Him after He was resurrected from the dead, they understood the importance of surrounding themselves with other believers.

Growing up, I always dreaded going to synagogue. However, when I began attending Messianic congregational services, I felt tremendous unity and tranquility at the gatherings. I began looking forward to the weekly Shabbat service that was filled with life, and was far more than simply reading prayers from a prayer book. I understand that your first attempt to get plugged into a faith community may not be as wonderful as mine was. But please, do not give up! We cannot do this alone—I strongly encourage anyone who wants to grow in his or her relationship and understanding of God to get plugged into a community of believers who truly love Yeshua.

> So there are many of us, and in union with the Messiah we comprise one body, with each of us belonging to the others. *Romans 12:5* [122]

Seek God continually, making prayer a part of your life. I find that the more I pray, the more vibrant and alive my relationship with God becomes.[123] Just as the glory and magnificence of heaven is unimaginable, so too is a relationship with God in your daily life. I continue to be in awe of the ways God works in my life.

> Don't worry about anything; on the contrary, make your requests known to God by prayer and petition, with thanksgiving. Then God's shalom (peace), passing all understanding, will keep your hearts and minds safe in union with the Messiah Yeshua, (parenthetical added). *Philippians 4:6-7* [124]

All too often, belief in Yeshua is confined to the idea that we want to believe in Him to get to Heaven. Although eternal joy rooted in an enduring relationship with our Creator in Heaven is *extremely important*, it is not the only blessing we can receive. I have experienced far more love and peace through my personal relationship with Yeshua than I ever could have imagined was possible. Understanding the grace of God, the depth of the sacrifice of Yeshua, and experiencing the comfort and wisdom of the Holy Spirit[125] far exceeds anything this world has to offer.[126] Like any relationship, it is an ongoing process. The more diligently we seek and honor Him, the more we learn and receive. As we grow in our relationship with God, our understanding of the fullness of His love likewise grows.

Yeshua is truly a God who is worthy of worship. After being tortured, humiliated, and betrayed, as Yeshua hung on the cross, He exhibited empathy and compassion for His enemies. He cried out to God and said, "Father forgive them, for they know not what they do," (Luke 23:34).[127] Yeshua, who performed many miracles, chose to endure a horrific death for the redemption of every one of us. What an amazing God!

If you have not accepted Yeshua as your LORD, I would encourage you to do so.[128] God wants to meet you right where you are. You do not have to clean up your life before you can come to Him. The Messiah Yeshua desires a personal relationship with you.

Is there any reason to wait?

ENDNOTES

1   Licona, Michael. *The Resurrection of Jesus: A New Historiographical Approach.* Downers Grove: InterVarsity Press, 2010. 68-69. Print.

2   As will be demonstrated in the following pages, these three historical individuals, though greatly historically attested, do not have *as much* historical evidence to support their lives as Yeshua does.

3   Licona, *The Resurrection of Jesus,* 68-69.

4   The 27 books of the New Covenant were chosen using four major criteria:

     1.   An apostle or a colleague of an apostle wrote the text

     2.   The text was orthodox (aligned with the teachings of Yeshua)

     3.   The material was relevant to the body of believers

     4.   There was a wide-spread and long-lasting usage of the text by the followers of Yeshua

    Licona, Michael. "How Did The Bible Become Compiled Into One Volume?" Houston University. n.d. Lecture.

5   There is some speculation regarding the authorship of the four gospels. However, after analyzing the evidence, many historians have no qualms with assigning each gospel to its traditionally named author.

    Papias wrote in approximately 125 CE that the Gospel of Mark "made no mistakes" in accurately recording Peter's eyewitness. Papias also records that Matthew had preserved the teachings of Yeshua correctly. This suggests two of the four gospels were verified to be historically accurate within the first century of the following of Yeshua.

Further, in 180 CE, Irenaeus, who was an early leader in the following of Yeshua, affirms the accurate recording and traditional authorship of all four gospels.

Strobel, Lee. *The Case for Christ*. Grand Rapids: Zondervan, 1998. 28-29. Print.

6   William Mitchell Ramsay was an early 20th century archaeologist and New Covenant scholar who was the leading authority on the history of Asia Minor. He writes this about Luke: "Luke is a historian of the first rank... This author should be placed along with the very greatest of historians."

Ramsay, William Mitchell. *The Bearing of Recent Discovery on the Trustworthiness of the New Testament*. Grand Rapids: Baker Book House, 1953. Print.

7   Bruce, F.F. *The New Testament Documents: Are They Reliable?* Grove: InterVarsity, 1960. Print.

These dates were also verified in *The Case for Christ* by Lee Strobel. During an interview with Craig Blomberg, Strobel recognizes Blomberg is "one of the country's foremost authorities on the biographies of Jesus, which are called the four gospels," (40).

Blomberg says, "The standard scholarly dating, even in very liberal circles, is Mark in the 70's, Matthew and Luke in the 80's, and John in the 90's," (40). Although the dates are slightly different than those proposed by Bruce and recorded in the text, the timeframe is still the same (35-70 years following the death of Yeshua), thus further affirming the historical credibility of the gospels.

Strobel, *The Case for Christ*, 40.

8   Strobel also recognizes just how expansive the post-resurrection testimonies would have been in a court of law. He writes: "To put it in perspective, if you were to call each one of the witnesses to a court of law to be cross-examined for just fifteen minutes each, and you went around the clock without a break, it would take you from breakfast on Monday until dinner on Friday to hear them all. After listening to 129 straight hours of eyewitness testimony, who could possibly walk away unconvinced?"

Strobel, *The Case for Christ*, 320.

The Apostle Paul likewise affirms that over 500 people at once saw the resurrected Yeshua: "And that He appeared to Cephas, then to the twelve. Then he appeared to more than *five hundred brothers at one time*, most of whom are still alive, though some have fallen asleep. Then He appeared to James, then to all the apostles. Last of all, as to one untimely born, he appeared also to me," (emphasis added), (1 Corinthians 15:5-8). Additional non-biblical evidence for the resurrection will be discussed throughout this booklet.

9   *Livius: Articles on Ancient History.* 2004. Web.

10 Schoville, Keith N. "Top Ten Archaeological Discoveries of the Twentieth Century Relating to the Biblical World." *Stone Campbell Journal* 4:1 (2002): n.pag. Web.

11 Licona, Michael. "The Basis of our Biblical Text Manuscripts." Houston Baptist University. n.d. Lecture.

12 "The New Testament, then, has not only survived in more manuscripts than any other book from antiquity, but it has survived in a purer form than any other great book— a form that is *99.5 percent pure*," (emphasis added).

Quoted in Lee Strobel's *The Case for Christ.*

Original quote by Norman L. Geisler, and William E. Nix. *A General Introduction to the Bible.* Chicago: Moody Press, 1980. 361. Print.

This point was also discussed during Licona's lecture *The Basis of our Biblical Text Manuscripts* given at Houston Baptist University.

13 Quoted in Josh McDowell, *The New Evidence that Demands a Verdict,* 34.

Original quote by John W. Montgomery. *History and Christianity.* Downers Grove: InterVarsity Press, 1971.

14 Brumbaugh, Robert S. "Plato Manuscripts: Toward a Completed Inventory." *Manuscripta,* July 1990. Web.

15 Matthew 28:2-7

16 John 20:12

17 For a more detailed look at perceived inaccuracies in the gospels, I recommend Dr. William Lane Craig's short Q&A article *Inerrancy and the Resurrection,* which can be found on his website reasonablefaith.org.

18 Licona, *The Resurrection of Jesus*, 235.

19 Quoted in G.J. Goldberg's *John the Baptist and Josephus.* Web.

Original quote by Josephus *Antiquities* 18.5.2.116.

20 Mark 6:27

21 Quoted in Michael Licona, *The Resurrection of Jesus,* 236.

Original quote translated by Meier (1994), 281.

22 Mark 6:2-3

23 Matthew 27:2

24   "Therefore, to squelch the rumor, Nero created scapegoats and subjected to the most refined tortures those whom the common people called "Christians," [a group] hated for their abominable crimes. Their name comes from Christ, who, during the reign of Tiberius, had been executed by the procurator Pontius Pilate. Suppressed for the moment, the deadly superstition broke out again, not only in Judea, the land which originated this evil, but also in the city of Rome."

Quoted in Michael Licona, *The Resurrection of Jesus*, 243.

Original quote by Tacitus, Ann. 15.44., 89-90.

25   "And when Pilate, because of an accusation made by the leading men among us, condemned him to the cross, those who had loved him previously did not cease to do so. And up until this very day the tribe of Christians [named after him] has not died out."

Quoted in Michael Licona, *The Resurrection of Jesus*, 239.

Original quote translated by Meier (1991), 61.

26   There are also references to Pilate in the writings of first century philosopher Philo of Alexandria.

27   Archeologists have discovered the inscription on the stone "not only confirms the historicity of Pilate, it clarifies the title that he bore as governor." This evidence coupled with the other writings of antiquity validate that Pontius Pilate is one of the best historically attested individuals in the crucifixion narrative.

Schoville, Keith N. "Top Ten Archaeological Discoveries of the Twentieth Century Relating to the Biblical World." *Stone Campbell Journal* 4:1 (2002): n.pag. Web.

28   The remains of a crucified man were discovered by Vassilios Tzaferis in 1968. In his Biblical Archaeology Review, Tzaferis writes, "He (the discovered crucified victim) was a Jew, of a good family, who may have been convicted of a political crime. He lived in Jerusalem shortly after the turn of the era and sometime before the Roman destruction of Jerusalem in 70 A.D.," (parenthetical added). This discovery confirms the gospel accounts that Yeshua could have been buried in a tomb after His crucifixion.

Tzaferis, Vassilios. "Crucifixion—The Archaeological Evidence." *Biblical Archaeology Review*, Jan/Feb 1985, 44-53.

29   Bruce, *The New Testament Documents: Are They Reliable*

30   Dr. Michael Licona has a fairly comprehensive list and analysis of the ancient adverse witnesses to the life and early following of Yeshua in his

book *The Resurrection of Jesus*, pages 235-248. His analysis (aside from the three witnesses described in the text: Josephus, the Babylonian Talmud, and Tacitus), includes the following sources:

1. The Roman Senator (and friend of Tacitus) Pliny the Younger wrote a letter to the Emperor Trajan (written around 111 CE).

2. The Roman historian Suetonius wrote a biography in which he mentioned early followers of Yeshua (written between 117-122 CE).

3. The Syrian Stoic Mara bar Serapion wrote a letter to his son from a Roman prison (written around 73 CE).

4. The historian Thallus affirmed information recorded in the New Covenant in his history of the eastern Mediterranean world (written around 55 CE).

5. In *The Passing of Peregrinus,* Lucian (who was a Syrian) referred to Yeshua (written around 165 CE).

6. The author Origen wrote an attack on Christianity (which will be discussed in further depth later in this booklet). (This work was written sometime between 177-180 CE.)

Although Josephus, the Babylonian Talmud, and Tacitus are not the only sources which affirm the life, death, and crucifixion of Yeshua, for our analysis, they have been deemed the most useful. If you are interested in this subject, I suggest further researching the above listed ancient sources.

Licona, *The Resurrection of Jesus*, 235.

[31] Quoted in Michael Licona, *The Resurrection of Jesus*, 239.

Original quote translated by Meier (1991), 61.

It should be noted that there is often a dispute regarding the authenticity of portions of this passage. Some scholars have noted that in some versions, it appears as if the original message may have been changed. However, the portion I have quoted in the text does not contain any of these disputed passages.

Further, Josephus' *Antiquities* were translated into Arabic which few of the early followers of Yeshua would have spoke. (In other words, the Church would not have had as much influence over being able to alter Josephus' original writings.) Thus, having duplicative fabrications of Josephus' writings would have been highly unlikely.

[32] Matthew 26:64

[33] Matthew 26:63-66

[34] John 19:31

As Lee Strobel confirms in *The Case for Christ*, breaking the legs of crucified victims would have sped up their death. Without the ability to push up and hold their weight with their legs, they would have died from asphyxiation within minutes, (268).

However, the soldiers discovered that Yeshua was already dead, so they did not break His legs. This fulfilled the messianic prophecy written hundreds of years in advance, "He keeps all of his bones, not one of them is broken," (Psalm 34:20).

[35] Quoted by Mark Eastman. *Blue Letter Bible.* Sowing Circle, n.d.. Web.

Original quote in b. Sanhedrin 43a.

Also quoted in Michael Licona, *The Resurrection of Jesus*, 247, with slightly different wording.

[36] Galatians 3:13, CJB

[37] Eastman, *Blue Letter Bible.*

[38] Quoted in Michael Licona, *The Resurrection of Jesus*, 243.

Original quote in Tacitus *Ann.* 15.44., 89-90.

[39] The Gospel of John offers excellent insight into the wisdom, love, and forgiveness of Yeshua. John records that Torah scholars and Pharisees (religious leaders) were ready to stone a woman caught in the act of committing adultery. In their minds, this was a necessary act in order to comply with their understanding of the Torah. Yeshua quieted this uprising with these simple words, "Let him who is without sin among you be the first to throw a stone at her," (John 8:7). The crowd laid down their stones and departed, one by one. Yeshua then exhorted the woman and said, "Neither do I condemn you; go, and from now on sin no more," (John 8:11). The gospels record the overwhelming mercy and compassion of Yeshua time and time again.

[40] John 5:17-18, 10:30-33, 14:1-9; 1 Timothy 3:16

[41] Mark 2:5-7

[42] Throughout this booklet, when referring to God as "**LORD**" all the letters will be capitalized. If you have read the Bible, you may have noticed that this is sometimes the case when "**LORD**" is used there as well.

In Exodus, God reveals His name. His name is translated into English as YHVH (the tetragrammaton), (Exodus 3:13-15). The ancient Israelites sought to preserve the sanctity of God's holy name so strictly, that they would not utter it aloud. Instead, they would pronounce God's name as "Adonai" which is a Hebrew word meaning Lord or Master.

So, anytime "**LORD**" is in all capital letters in the Bible or ancient Hebrew texts, it is a reference to YHVH or God. Anytime it is not in all capitals, it can also be also referring to God, or to a lord or master (the context of the verse is important for this distinction).

43   Lewis, C.S. *Mere Christianity.* New York: MacMillan Publishers. 1952. Print.

44   Just two examples of Jewish leaders who have acknowledged that Yeshua was a brilliant rabbi and a righteous man are Rabbi Shmuley Boteach and renowned Harvard Law Professor Alan Dershowitz.

Rabbi Boteach is a media personality who has authored the popular book *Kosher Jesus.* He writes, "There are many reasons for accepting Jesus as a man of great wisdom, beautiful ethical teachings, and profound Jewish patriotism."

Alan Dershowitz is a renowned Harvard Law Professor. In a CNN interview on April 7, 2000, Professor Dershowitz echoed the sentiments of Rabbi Boteach. He said, "I think of Jesus as the first reform rabbi, a wonderful teacher, who tried to make Judaism less formalistic and more ethical."

Boteach, Shmuley. *Kosher Jesus.* Jerusalem: Gefen, 2012. Print.

45   Matthew 28:17

46   Keller, Timothy. *The Reason for God.* New York: Penguin Group, 2008. 88. Print.

47   Perhaps one day medical science will be able to verify that resurrections are possible.

48   Newport, Frank. "More Than 9 in 10 Americans Continue to Believe in God." *Gallup Headlines.* Gallup, Inc., 3 June 2011. Web.; "Religion and the Unaffiliated." *Pew Research Centers Religion Public Life.* Pew Research Center, 8 Oct. 2012. Web.

49   Dr. Francis Collins, one of the core leaders of the Human Genome Project, writes in his book *The Language of God* how important it is to have a "healthy skepticism" with regards to miraculous events. He writes: "Whatever the personal view, it is crucial that a healthy skepticism be applied when interpreting potentially miraculous events, lest the integrity and rationality of the religious perspective be brought into question." In other words, claims of a miraculous event should not be taken lightly.

50   Below are some of the miracles of Elisha recorded in the Old Covenant:

2 Kings

2:14- The Jordan river divided

4:35- After praying to God, Elisha raised a child from dead

4:43- Bread multiplied

6:17- Sight to the blind

13:21- Man comes to life by touching Elisha's bones

[51] Keener, Craig S. *Miracles: The Credibility of the New Testament Accounts.* Grand Rapids: Baker Academic, 2011. Print.

[52] Although *The True Word* manuscript has yet to be discovered (and may never be), it is quoted at length in the rebuttal *Contra Celsum*, written by Origen of Alexandria in the third century.

[53] Quoted by Peter Kirby. "Historical Jesus Theories." *Early Christian Writings.* 2015.

Original quote in *Contra Celsum, Ch. XXXVIII.*

[54] Just a reminder, an adverse witness is someone who disagrees with your overall position. In a courtroom, favorable testimony from an adverse witness is considered persuasive, as such a witness is certainly not going to lie or exaggerate to help your case.

[55] Quoted by Mark Eastman. *Blue Letter Bible.* Sowing Circle, n.d.. Web.

Original quote in b. Sanhedrin 43a.

Also quoted in Michael Licona, *The Resurrection of Jesus*, 247, with slightly different wording.

[56] Licona, *The Resurrection of Jesus*, 283.

[57] They "forsook Him and fled," (Mark 14:50), and returned to their old profession as fishermen (John 21:2-3).

[58] "And when Pilate, because of an accusation made by the leading men among us, condemned him to the cross, those who had loved him previously did not cease to do so. And up until this very day the tribe of Christians [named after him] has not died out."

Quoted in Michael Licona, *The Resurrection of Jesus*, 239.

Original quote translated by Meier (1991), 61.

[59] Quoted in Josh McDowell. *Evidence that Demands a Verdict: Historical Evidences for the Christian Faith.* San Bernardino: Here's Life Publishers, 1981. 244. Print.

Originally quoted in Pannenberg, Wolfhart. *Jesus: God and Man.* Trans. by L.L. Wilkins and D.A. Priebe. Philadelphia: Westminster Press, 1968.

[60] Wright, N.T. "The New Unimproved Jesus." *Christianity Today.* 13 Sept. 1993.

[61] "'I adjure you by the living God to tell us if you are the Christ, the *Son of God.*' Jesus said to him, 'You have said so. But I tell you, from now on you will see the Son of Man seated at the right hand of Power and coming on

the clouds of heaven.' Then the high priest tore his robes and said, 'He has uttered blasphemy,'" (emphasis added), (Matthew 26:63-65).

62   Matthew 27:11-26

63   Undoubtedly, this would probably not have included the Romans holding the hands of any doubters and politely showing them that they were incorrect. It would have been more akin to putting the brutalized corpse of Yeshua out in the public square for everyone to see.

64   It seems as if Yeshua's body were still lying in His tomb, thousands would not have been convinced of His resurrection. Acts 2 describes Peter's first sermon (which was given shortly after the resurrection of Yeshua) in which Peter unabashedly proclaims Yeshua lived, was crucified, died, buried, and resurrected by God. It is recorded that about 3,000 people came to believe in the resurrection of Yeshua that day, (Acts 2:41). Please also refer to Matthew 28:11-15 quoted in the text.

65   "Ancient Rome—The Pax Romana." *U.S. History.* Ancient Civilizations. Independence Hall Association. n.d. Web.

66   Matthew 28:11-15

67   Some may wonder what happened to the Roman soldiers during the resurrection of Yeshua. The Gospel of Matthew records that after an angel appeared at the tomb to tell the women that Yeshua had been resurrected, the guards were terrified. "And for fear of him (the angel) the guards trembled and became like dead men," (parenthetical added), (Matthew 28:4).

68   McDowell, *The New Evidence that Demands a Verdict,* 237.

69   Barney Fife was a bumbling deputy on the Andy Griffith TV Series in the 1960s. Chief Wiggum is an incompetent police officer on The Simpsons.

70   Matthew 6:33

71   Matthew 12:40, 16:21

72   Matthew 27:65-66

73   Mark 16:1-4

74   Quoted in Josh McDowell, *The New Evidence that Demands a Verdict,* 237. Original material found in Robertson, Archibald Thomas. *Word Pictures in the New Testament.* Vols. I-V. Nashville: Broadman Press, 1930. Reprint, New York: R.R. Smith, Inc., 1931.

75   Van Daalen, D.H. *The Real Resurrection.* London: Collins, 1972. 41. Print.

76   Craig, William Lane. "Accounting for the Empty Tomb: The Quest for the Risen, Historical Jesus." *American,* n.p., 1 Apr. 2013. Web.

77   Luke 23:50-53; John 19:38-40

78   Despite the *recent* controversy surrounding the life of Mary Magdalene (from such books as *The Da Vinci Code),* she is still an important figure in the resurrection story.

    If you find *The Da Vinci Code* controversy interesting, I would suggest either listening to or reading through the transcript of the "DaVinci Code Forum" hosted by the Johnson Ferry Baptist Church in Marietta, Georgia. The two scholars in this forum are Dr. William Lane Craig and Dr. Michael Licona. They debunk the conspiracies regarding Mary Magdalene in a succinct and comprehensive manner. This forum can be found on Dr. Craig's website, *Reasonable Faith with William Lane Craig.*

79   Mark 15:47, 16:1-3

80   Mark 15:44-45

81   McDowell, *The New Evidence that Demands a Verdict,* 281.

82   John 19:39-40

83   John 19:34

84   Edwards, William D., Wesley J. Gabel, and Floyd E. Hosmer. "On the Physical Death of Jesus Christ." *The Journal of the American Medical Association.* 255.20, 1986. Web.

85   Paul says that he studied under Gamaliel, one of the chief rabbis of the day, (Acts 22:3).

86   Acts 22:20

87   Acts 9:1-22

88   There is debate among some scholars as to whether all of the following letters were authored by Paul. Notably, there is virtually no debate over Paul's authorship of 7 letters (*). However, the full list of the traditional 13 Pauline Epistles (writings/letters) is: Romans*, 1 Corinthians*, 2 Corinthians*, Galatians*, Ephesians, Philippians*, Colossians, 1 Thessalonians*, 2 Thessalonians, 1 Timothy, 2 Timothy, Titus, Philemon*

89   1 Corinthians 15:6

90   In *The Resurrection of Jesus,* Dr. Licona writes: "It is believed that Paul wrote the letter we now refer to as 1 Corinthians in A.D. 54 or 55. If Jesus died in A.D. 30, we are reading a letter that was written within twenty-five years of Jesus' death by a major church leader who knew a number of those who had walked with Jesus," (223).

91   1 Corinthians 15:3-8

92   Galatians 1:13-14

93   Strobel, *The Case for Christ*, 322.

94   Licona, *The Resurrection of Jesus*, 370.

95   Time and time again it is written in the texts of the New Covenant that these are accounts from *eyewitnesses*. This means that the writers would have known if what they were writing was historically true or false. "For we did not follow cleverly devised myths when we made known to you the power and coming of our Lord Jesus Christ, but we were eyewitnesses of his majesty," (2 Peter 1:16).

96   "How happy is its church, on which apostles poured forth all their doctrine along with their blood! Where Peter endures a passion like his Lord's! Where Paul wins his crown in a death like John's! Where the Apostle John was first plunged, unhurt, into boiling oil, and thence remitted to his island-exile!"

      "Ante-Nicene Fathers, Vol. III: The Prescription Against Heretics." *Christian Classics Electronic Library.* Chap XXXVI. 1998. Web.

97   The Jewish population would have taken the claim that Yeshua was the Son of God very seriously. The first of the 10 Commandments given to Moses on Mount Sinai is to worship "no other Gods," (Exodus 20:3; Deuteronomy 5:7).

      Some Jews to this day do not accept Yeshua as the Messiah because of their interpretation of this commandment. As is discussed in depth in chapter 7 of my book *A Lawyer's Case for His Faith*, the evidence that Yeshua is the Jewish Messiah and the Son of God is overwhelming. This means that the followers of Yeshua understand that they are worshipping God, not an idol or a man.

98   Ludemann, Gerd. *What Really Happened to Jesus: A Historical Approach to the Resurrection.* trans. John Bowden. Louisville: Westminster John Knox Press, 1996. 8. Print.

99   There are an estimated *2.2 billion* believers in Yeshua today.

      Chappell, Bill. "World's Muslim Population Will Surpass Christians This Century, Pew Says." *NPR*. NPR, 2 Apr. 2015. Web.

100   Durant, Will. *Caesar and Christ.* Vol. 3. New York: Simon & Schuster, 1994. Print.

101   Mark 3:13-19 lists the names of the 12 disciples before the crucifixion of Yeshua.

102   Mark 15:42-46; Matthew 27:57-60; Luke 23:50-53; John 19:38

103   Matthew 28:1-10; Mark 16:1-8; Luke 23:55; 24:1-12; John 20:1-2

104   Habermas, "The Empty Tomb of Jesus." *Evidence for God*, 169.

[105] Dr. William Lane Craig reiterates that "one of the most remarkable facts about the early Christian belief in Jesus' resurrection was that it flourished in the very city where Jesus had been publicly crucified."

Craig, *Reasonable Faith*, 361.

[106] It is recorded that Paul preached in Jerusalem (Acts 26:20).

[107] Mark 14:50

[108] Mark 14:66-72

[109] Acts 2

[110] "Ante-Nicene Fathers, Vol. III: The Prescription Against Heretics." Chap XXXVI.

[111] John 21:2-3

[112] McDowell, *The Evidence that Demands a New Verdict*, 252.

[113] The fact that Yeshua's following is still in existence (and continues to grow) is even more impressive after taking into account the other followings that began during that time period. The Book of Acts records that during an exchange among the members of the Jewish Council shortly after Yeshua's death Gamaliel, a highly esteemed Pharisee, describes several recent self-proclaimed messiahs who had prompted short-lived followings. After each of these proclaimed messiahs were killed, their following disbanded. Gamaliel advises the council to leave the followers of Yeshua alone. He reasons that if Yeshua is not the Messiah, His following will quickly dissolve. But conversely he notes that, "If it is of God, you will not be able to overthrow them," (Acts 5:39). Regardless of whether you believe in the historicity of the New Covenant, the logic and rendition of historical events proposed by Gamaliel is sound. If there were other individuals during this time who claimed to be the Messiah and their followings all disbanded, why is the following of Yeshua still widely impactful? There are an estimated *2.2 billion* believers in Yeshua today. It is clear that even from the beginning, there has been something very different about the following of Yeshua.

[114] Maier, Paul L. *In the Fullness of Time: A Historian Looks at Christmas, Easter, and the Early Church*. Grand Rapids: Kregel Publications, 1997. 203. Print.

[115] "And if the Messiah has not been raised, your trust is useless, and you are still in your sins," (1 Corinthians 15:17, CJB).

[116] Green, Michael. *Man Alive*. Chicago: InterVarsity Christian Fellowship, 1969. 54. Print.

Epilogue

[117] My book *A Lawyer's Case for His Faith* has more information about the incredible historical evidence for the resurrection of Yeshua, as well as other foundational topics (e.g., the evidence for the existence of God, whether the Bible can be used as historical evidence, and the evidence that Yeshua is the prophesied Jewish Messiah).

[118] Job 26:14

[119] Jeremiah 29:13

[120] 2 Timothy 3:16

Even if you do not believe the Bible is the inspired Word of God, it is still an invaluable tool with tremendous insights for life.

[121] Acts 2:44-47

[122] Romans 12:5, CJB

[123] During prayer time, God often speaks silently to our hearts and minds. The Old Covenant refers to this as God's "still small voice," (1 Kings 19:12).

[124] Philippians 4:6-7, CJB

[125] Ruakh HaKodesh is Hebrew for the Holy Spirit.

The Holy Spirit is the Spirit of God that we can invite to reside in us to be our Comforter and Guide.

"But you will receive power when the Holy Spirit has come upon you, and you will be my witnesses in Jerusalem and in all Judea and Samaria, and to the end of the earth," (Acts 1:8).

"And who has also put his seal on us and given us his Spirit in our hearts as a guarantee," (2 Corinthians 1:22).

For a more in-depth discussion about the triune nature of God, please refer to Chapter 7 in my book *A Lawyer's Case for His Faith*.

[126] 1 Timothy 6:7

Wealth, power, and prestige are fleeting, but the love of God is enduring forever.

[127] Luke 23:34

[128] Here is a suggestion of a short prayer, similar to the prayer I prayed over 23 years ago:

God, I want to know if you are real. Please give me a better understanding of you. Help the Bible come alive to me so that I better see your plan of salvation through your Son, Yeshua. In Yeshua's name I pray, Amen.

This prayer is modeled after Ephesians 1:15-23, in which Paul prayed this for others.

"For this reason, ever since I heard about your trust in the Lord Yeshua and your love for all God's people, I have not stopped giving thanks for you. In my prayers I keep asking the God of our Lord Yeshua the Messiah, the glorious Father, to give you a spirit of wisdom and revelation, so that you will have full knowledge of him. I pray that he will give light to the eyes of your hearts, so that you will understand the hope to which he has called you, what rich glories there are in the inheritance he has promised his people, and how surpassingly great is his power working in us who trust him. It works with the same mighty strength he used. when he worked in the Messiah to raise him from the dead and seat him at his right hand in heaven, far above every ruler, authority, power, dominion or any other name that can be named either in the 'olam hazeh or in the 'olam haba. Also, he has put all things under his feet and made him head over everything for the Messianic Community, which is his body, the full expression of him who fills all creation," (Ephesians 1:15-23, CJB).

ACKNOWLEDGMENTS

I would like to thank my amazing wife, Cathy, for her patience, prayers, and love throughout our 35 years of marriage. Her modeling of God's unconditional love has drawn me to want to know Him more. Knowing her has been one of the greatest gifts I have ever received. Her help (and patience) with this booklet has been absolutely invaluable. Researching and writing this booklet has truly been a labor of love.

I also want to thank my children who have inspired me greatly over the years. They are a tremendous blessing! They all had very helpful suggestions to make this book more impactful. I am also grateful to Rabbi Don Goldstein, Rabbi Shmuel Wolkenfeld, Amy Adler, and others who assisted with the research and writing of this booklet. A special shout-out to Cara Strike who worked tirelessly on this for a year and a half.

I am also thankful to God for His protection, patience, and unconditional, everlasting love. How comforting is it to know that as I sojourn through life, He is with me 24/7. He has graciously forgiven me and allowed me to experience the depths of His love, which I never knew existed until I was 39 years old.

I want to also thank my mother, brother, sister, and stepfather for the impact they have had on my life. My father passed away from lung cancer when I was 10, and my mother was suddenly faced with the daunting challenge of raising three young children alone. She masterfully accomplished this task while working full-time. She made innumerable sacrifices that have continued to be a blessing in my life. She eventually married my stepfather who helped to raise my siblings and me. My stepfather treated me like his own son. Without his constant support, I do not believe I would be a lawyer today.

Growing up, I was very close to my older sister and brother. I moved from St. Louis to Kansas City, and during my visits to my hometown, my sister was *always* a gracious hostess, and has played a big role in creating many family memories. My brother, who is also a lawyer, has imparted many words of "fatherly" advice and wisdom that have significantly influenced the direction of my life. My family has been, and will always be, a huge blessing in my life. I love them all dearly.

ABOUT THE AUTHOR

Jim Jacob has been a senior partner at his law firm since 1979. He has been privileged to represent prominent civic leaders, large U.S. companies, and countless individuals. For many years, Jim has held the highest rating from Martindale-Hubbell, a prominent company that evaluates lawyers nationwide. Jim has been admitted to practice law before the United States Supreme Court, and was selected for membership to Outstanding Lawyers of America. Jim has written articles on legal topics for both the *Kansas City Star* and *Missouri Lawyers Weekly*.

Jim's first book, *A Lawyer's Case for God*, has received international acclaim and has been translated into three languages. The contents of this booklet are an abbreviated version of three chapters in Jim's book, *A Lawyer's Case for His Faith*.

Jim and his wife, Cathy, have been married for 35 years and have four children. Jim and Cathy have served for many years in varying leadership roles at their congregation. Jim also serves two international not-for-profit organizations—one as a legal advisor, and one as a board member and officer.